To Shirley.
with all my love

from Gloria

May 2006.

This Book
Belongs to

Shirley
Scully.

CYCLAMEN © Gay Corran 1986

Maggie Humphry's

SHROPSHIRE

A pictorial record
of this beautiful
and historic county
as seen through the eyes
of professional artist
Maggie Humphry

Maggie Humphry's

SHROPSHIRE

Published by
GET Publishing, The Old Fire Engine Station, 1 High Street, Bridgnorth, Shropshire WV16 4DB

shropshire@getservices.org.uk

First published 2004

ISBN 0-9548793-0-9

Printed in the United Kingdom by Cambrian Printers, Ceredigion, SY23 3TN

Thanks to the lovely friendly people of Shropshire for allowing me to sit and draw in their fields, gardens, farms and forecourts, and for all the mugs of tea.
Thanks also to everyone who helped, supported and encouraged me.

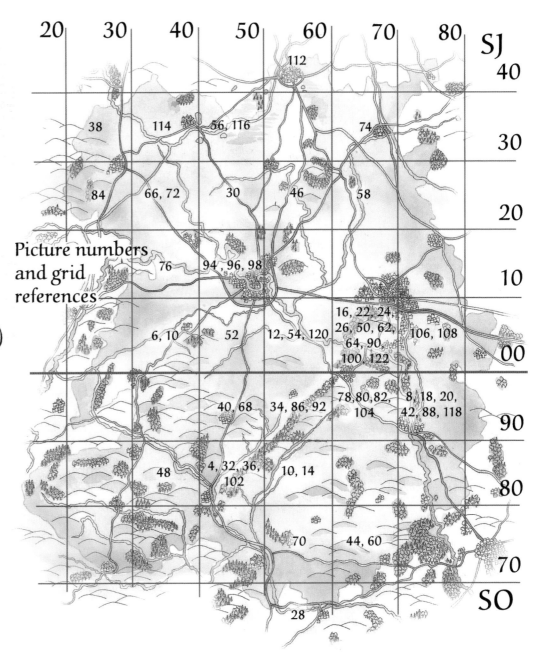

Picture numbers and grid references

Introducing Maggie Humphry

Associate of Royal Birmingham Society of Artists

Maggie started her training at St. Albans School of Art. Whilst there she had the good fortune to meet Quentin Crisp, a regular model. He told her to "always do things with style, my dear": and she's tried.

She went on to teacher training at Swansea School of Art & University and became head of an art department in her early twenties. After just a few years as a teacher, she decided to take the leap into independence as a professional artist. She was at that time a Fellow of Digswell House at Welwyn Garden City, and gained enormously from her close contact with such innovative and notable colleagues as John Brunsdon (etcher), Peter Collingwood (weaver), and Mick & Sheila Casson (ceramicists).

For many years Maggie lived near Ruthin in North Wales, becoming very well known as a ceramicist. Her enormous output during 30 years of work included highly collectable delicate, distinctive figures, and large ceramic murals in public places. She created many murals to commission in England and Wales and there's even one in Nazareth. Examples of her highly individual and immensely detailed work can be seen on walls in Ruthin, Rhyl, Bangor, Ness Gardens, Barmouth's Dragon Theatre, Kingston-upon-Thames, Holyhead, Liverpool, and Wigan Court House (which Maggie was very proud to see unveiled by Lady Diana, Princess of Wales).

The pictures in this book

As anyone who's worked in clay will know very well, it's heavy stuff. It eventually took its toll on Maggie, as it does on so many ceramicists, and so in 1993 she left the clay aside and began to retrace her steps towards drawing, painting and etching. Of these, her major love is drawing. Of course, she's really been doing it for ages, since all her ceramic pieces began their lives as designs on paper.

The sixty main images in this collection cover all parts of Shropshire, capturing its magic in different ways. Each is taken from an original drawing in pen & ink, worked up with watercolours. They're all very complex, dedicated works that look so simple: but that's Maggie's skill. Each one is a pleasure to look at as a picture, but when you look closely, you can see the high quality, precise work that creates the overall impression.

Maggie doesn't use a sketchbook, nor does she take many photographs. All these drawings began life stuck to a board with masking tape whilst she sat with her pens in field, street, or courtyard. So they reflect her own way of seeing, and every one is enriched with its personal, idiosyncratic perspective from the first few lines through to the diligent working-up in the studio.

Maggie always has been sensitive to the small details that are such a core part of our world. She notices the shapes and shadows of buildings, whether they be farms or churches, power stations, pubs or simply places to live. She always has had a meticulous concern to convey expression, and to achieve a proper balance of colour, shape, and form. She's also keen to keep her art "alive", so frequently includes either people or their animals: and they're often fun.

If there is a heaven for me, it is sitting in a field in the sun drawing picturesque buildings.

From Wales I moved to Shropshire, whose charm and softness has totally beguiled me: a cornucopia overflowing with everything that excites me visually. The flat wet lands to the north where once windmills turned in abundance and where herons stand in pools, the hills in the south rubbing shoulders with Wales, grazed by surefooted sheep. Cornfields splashed with poppies, woods where deer hide in the day and owls reign by night. Farms and barns and swallows, rivers and rolling hills. But it is the buildings that attract me most.

Villages crammed with boundless, luscious architectural gems having evaded the ravages of redevelopment. Towns where mediaeval houses cluster at crazy angles round castles, the half timbered butting up to the old sandstone. Where colourful markets have filled the streets for centuries.

It is all so English and I love it. Perhaps the many years that I lived in the land of the dragon has made me appreciate this rural English county even more.

"What should they know of England who only England know".
Like Kipling my enchantment is total.

Thousands of our magnificent English Shire horses were killed alongside our young men in the trenches of the First World War. Afterwards these sturdy Percherons were brought across from France to work the English soil.

The Dawkins scratch in the farmyard, and country sounds rise from barns, dairy and meadow — a step back in time.

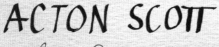

ACTON SCOTT

4

working farm museum

SO 458.896

Restored over decades this magnificent creature is alive once more. It reminds me of a song that we sang, in our triple descant voices, at school. "Behold a giant am I, aloft here in my tower", about a windmill which "devoured the wheat, the maize and the rye".

The stern west wind, with the chill of winter still in its threads, stirred the sails, tugged at my paper and bit through my padded coat. Then delightfully tossed the first swallow of spring over my head.

6	**ASTERLEY** windmill

SJ 373.076

Picked in her summer garden and carefully sewn into tiny muslin bags gathered with a satin ribbon, my grandmother's lavender scented the drawers of my childhood.

| 8 | **ASTLEY ABBOTTS**
lavender farm
<div align="center">SO 706. 964</div> |

Poplar   Pine

© Maggie Humphry

"There's not a straight line in it" said the landlord as he sat down on the bank watching me and looking at his property.

His car park was once a quarry and being part of Wenlock Edge, trilobites and other limestone fossils have been lying in the dark for 425 million years. On a cold day it's difficult to imagine it was once in tropical waters.

10	ASTON MUNSLOW
	the Swan pub
	SO 513.867

© Maggie Humphry

1:39   D. wood moves   Malcolm Williams publican   The Swan. Aston Munslow

Sand martins nest in the river bank, and deep in the autumn woods the toadstools sprout in the damp leaf litter.

With the freedom of childhood I roamed the woods. I knew where the foxes earth was and where the most exotic fungi grew, so it was with disbelief that the only time I went to Brownies I found that I had to dance round a giant plastic mushroom! Me, who climbed the tallest trees and jumped through high flames of stolen straw thrown on our campfire.

12	ATTINGHAM
	cows in the park
	SJ 551. 100

I learnt to swim with eyes open in the murky seas of Cornwall
Here now, like living under water, these grey buildings and grey winter skies.
Suddenly a shoal of white doves swim by.

14	**BEAMBRIDGE** Temple Farm Dovecot SO 529.883

Another place full of haunting atmosphere. Native honey bees nest in the vicinity and occupied the sundial at onetime.

The scrapping badgers left tufts of hair wet by the morning dew.

16	**BENTHALL** St. Bartholomew's church SJ 658.026

Originally built for Low Town workers, the Cliff railway stills thrills both young and old, and many a friend and family member of mine is given 'the treat'.

As you descend the damp 'cut' where ferns and liverwort cling, remember you are travelling through desert sand dunes formed 250 million years ago.

| 18 | **BRIDGNORTH**
Cliff Railway
SO 728.929 |

Tumbling down a narrow wooded valley the stream has worked this wonderful iron wheel for 300 years. Willow trees drip into the pool and swallows skim across the glassy surface.

| 20 | **BRIDGNORTH**
Daniel's Mill
SO 718.917 |

©Ann too [illegible] [illegible] [illegible] [illegible] [illegible]   BY Maggie Humphry

No need to spend on a P.R. course, just sit on the corner chair for a couple of hours and learn how to treat people. The hub of the town full of chatter and laughter cheers the heart on a gloomy day.

| 22 | **BROSELEY**
the Greengrocer
SJ 674.016 |

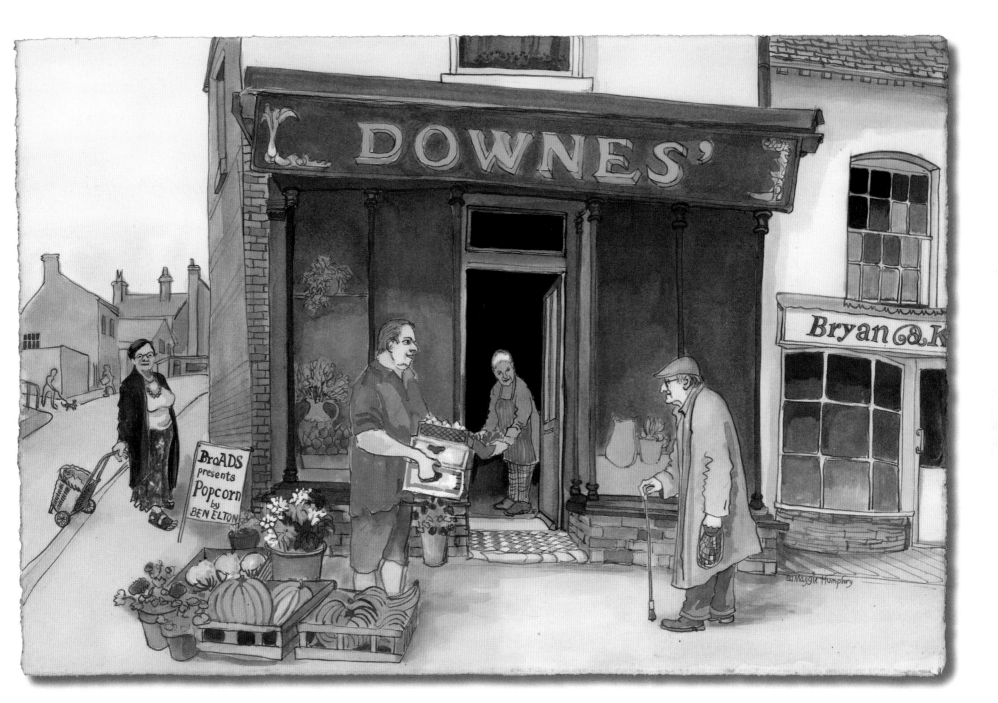

BINDWEED
by Marilyn Gunn
(Allotment Queen)

You own the ground:
not just taking it once
but breaking forwards, backwards
with a strangling force
that keeps your bloodless knuckles clenched.

You don't give in
without a fight:
I beat the earth away
but still your fingers cling,
brittle and miserly,
driven by longings
blanched by a loss of ownership.

24	**BROSELEY**
	Chapel Allotments
	SJ 671.018

Children's playground calls echo across the flood plain whilst docile Daisy the longhorn grazes on the banks of the river Severn. Since pesticides were banned the otter population has grown from strength to strength on the river Severn and may be seen when their holts are flooded with rising water.

| 26 | **BUILDWAS**
The Primary School
SJ 636.046 |

BUILDWAS
PRIMARY
SCHOOL

the vanes turn idly in the breeze. No smell of drying hops hangs in the air now. Yet behind in the orchard the apple trees still drown with white blossom in spring and in the autumn bow their branches down with heavy fruit.

28	**BURFORD**
	Lockyers Farm
	SO 585.685

© Maggie Humphry

A feast for the eyes to see so many wonderful objects.

At my concern the owner kindly broke a window to let out all the newly hatched green bumble bees which were beating against the glass in search of freedom.

Bumble bees love poppies but you have to catch them early as by lunchtime all the pollen has been taken.

BURLTON

North Shropshire
Reclamation Centre   SJ 443.278

A magical place on a summers eve with the scent of bluebells heavy in the air and cuckoos calling into the dusk.

Once these woods rang to the sound of coppicing axes of men long since gone and the smoke of the charcoal burners. Now a great spotted woodpecker climbs slowly picking dinner on the open arms of the tree. I sit still.

32	**BUSHMOOR**
	Coppice

SO 431·880

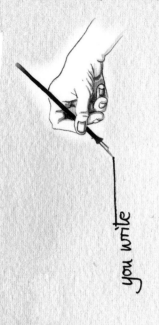

you write

Cardington is bursting at the seams with wondrous architecture but it was these boots stuffed with flowers which tickled my fancy. Having trudged up and down the vegetable patch for many a long year, they end their days in floral splendour on the cottage wall.

34	**CARDINGTON**
	Boots
	SO 504.953

This exciting mediaeval building has seen a host of golden harvests packed into its wooden walls. The staddlestones are six feet high down the slope, but a foot is not far for a rat to jump at the top end.

The Onny Trail at Cheyney Longville is internationally important for geology.

36	**CHENEY LONGVILLE**
	Castle Farm
	SO 416.847

With one foot still in England these two lovely giants together leap the river and stride off to Wales.

Croeso i Gymru. Mae'n rhaid i ti siarad Cymraeg 'rwan.

38	**CHIRK** Viaduct
	SJ 287.373

Once a speciality of South Shropshire hill tops the yellow Mountain pansy declined due to agriculture. But in 2001, because of the Foot and Mouth disease, the animals and walkers were taken off the Long Mynd and this little flower flourished once more.

Heart's ease.
Love in idleness.
Two old names for the pansy.

40	CHURCH STRETTON
	SO 456:936

© Maggie Humphry

ANTIQUES

The church of All Saints has the most exciting interior I have seen in Shropshire. The 13th century murals being the plum in the architectural pie. Infact all the buildings in Claverley are delicious enough to eat.

42 | CLAVERLEY

SO 793.933

Anne Kinsey   Shaw Lane Albrighton.   WV7 3DS.

There seemed to be a greenfinch calling from every garden, and bright butterflies flitting. Infact the warm spring sunshine woke enough butterflies to take the church heavenwards. I rescued 23 (19 tortoiseshells, 2 peacocks, and a comma). As well as a flower rota, I think the church should have a butterfly rota.

The only other twisted spire I know is Chesterfield.

44	CLEOBURY MORTIMER
	SO 676.756

Greenfinch in c... Maggie Humphreys

At the foot of the church a solid stone cart track leads up to the hill top where, to restore the old heathland, heather and bilberry are being planted.

Showing its age, the top shaley layer of rocks contain rhynchasaurus footprints.

46	**CLIVE AND GRINSHILL** Hope Farm SJ 513.233

Formerly the 'Pig and Whistle' and before that 'the Raven' public house, Dutch cottage now displays a dazzling new hair cut. A straw deer (the thatcher's symbol) lies across the roof ridge on the far side, sprouting real stag horns.

In the wee hamlet of Pentre Hodre nearby lies a pool containing great crested newts. In Wales, I made a small pond into which came the common and palmate newts. They will eat frog tadpoles but not toad tadpoles, I observed. Digging a much larger pond in the hope that great crested newts would be attracted, I was rewarded 5 years later when one large male turned up. He obviously had charisma, as the following year 2 females arrived. When I left Wales there were 15, including the 'teenagers' who had been born there. Great crested newts will eat both frog and toad tadpoles, dragonfly lavae, and anything small that moves, even bits of minced meat which I used to roll down the side of the pond. Infact, if you are not careful they will eat you out of house and ~~home~~ pond.

48 | **CLUNBURY**
Dutch Cottage
SO 371 . 806

Maggie Humphry ©

How lovely to see the old woodland crafts continued. Gentle people, including a little Welsh man (with a song in his throat). I like to think that he floated down the river from the mountains in a coracle to start work where he landed. You can make your own coracle here and what better way to see the river creatures, including the club tailed dragonfly (a speciality of the River Severn and Thames), than floating quietly down stream. What was it Ratty said in the 'Wind in the Willows'? — "theres nothing like messing about in boats".

| 50 | **COALBROOKDALE** the Greenwood Trust

SJ 667.038 |

wooden shingles   sue challis = director   gerwyn mary = wendli

Maggie Humphry '15

Called by the proclaiming church bells a gaggle of wonderful hats paraded past me. Shame they are worn only for weddings.

Having slipped into a kettle hole in the ice, the most complete skeleton of a mammoth was found in the sand and gravel here.

| 52 | **CONDOVER**
the Old Vicarage
SJ 495.058 |

wedding-hats   The Old Vicarage Gardens

People laugh when they see this picture, but I had just drawn this barn and returning home heard the news of some pigs that had run from the gunmen who'd been ordered to slaughter them because of the Foot and Mouth disease. So as a memorial I have put them in my picture. So many of our fields are empty of animals now.

54	CROSS HOUSES
	Pigs at Black Barn
	SJ 552.063

From the 300 year old bowling green I spied this sunny garden below.
Whilst bird feeders buldged, fat little tits feigning starvation flitted round my head.

56	**ELLESMERE** the artists garden
	SJ 403.347

© Maggie Humphry

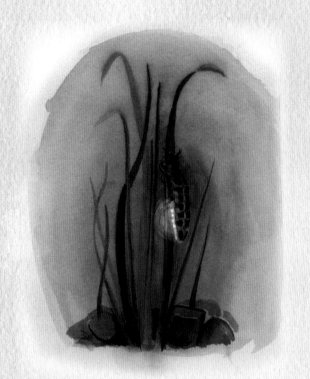

A nocturnal search reveals glow worms, a magical little insect not seen since childhood. They are attracted by the ballast on the disused railway line near this pretty village.

58	HODNET
	SJ 613. 286

All made of different materials, this group of houses is as delightful as the village name.

60 | HOPTON WAFERS

SO 637.762

© Maggie Humphry

The red evening sky against the chimneys Echos the famous oil painting by Philip James de Loutherbourg of Coalbrookdale in all its industrial glory. Wonderful roaring colours singing in the skies.

There being no natural cliffs in Shropshire a cooling tower would act as the perfect place for the peregrine falcon box that the Shropshire Wildlife Trust made. But a local "pigeon fancier" threatened a lawsuit if one of his precious birds was eaten. So it wasn't installed. The box was taken instead to Derbyshire to be put up in a cement works quarry. Shame, I say.

IRONBRIDGE

62

Chimneys

SJ 658.036

Maggie Humphry

Yes I really did sit here in the snow: in a sleeping bag with my feet on a hot water bottle! When snow flurries came I put my board upside down on my head to keep the drawing dry.

you write

64 | IRONBRIDGE

SJ 673.034

Weighing it up!

66	KNOCKIN
	Shop
	SJ 332.223

I know a cave where the bats hang by day. I am always pleased to see the first bat of the evening flitting around as the sun disappears behind the hill. A female pipistrelle with young will catch 3,000 mosquitos and midges a night.

| 68 | **LITTLE STRETTON**
All Saints Church
SO 443.918 |

© Maggie Humphry

The bustle in the market square subsides as evening approaches, and the townsfolk head homewards, clutching their goodies. Salmon jump in the river Teme. Many times in summer I row one of the wee municipal boats up stream amongst the cornfields. The best view of the castle is from a boat.

LUDLOW
the Southgate

70

SO 512 . 743

craven arms.   Lower dinchope barn (15)

The children are warmly welcomed after school for their club, and many an exciting project is worked on in this tin church "......and when that rains that don't 'arf rattle" (Bernard Miles)

In the field behind, the black crows (crow black, slow, black) pick at the cow pats with solid voices and lazy flap of wing. Many a fish head or fatty gristle I have offered to the couple which nest in a holly tree on the way to Much Wenlock. I once strung up a dead crow with nylon thread so that I could draw it from beneath. The smell of dead crow is quite sweet.

In his next life my brother wants to come back as a crow!

72	**MAESBURY**
	St. John the Baptist
	SJ 310. 257

1914 - 1919

A picturesque corner showing the
old grammar school where 'Clive of India' was a
pupil. He is reputed to have had a disagreement
with the owner of the shop next door so out of spite
one downpour diverted the running rain water into his cellar.

74	**MARKET DRAYTON** Old Grammar School SJ 676.341

J.H.Barber

© Maggie Humphry

Just stand on the door step and you can lob a pebble across the river Vyrnwy into Wales (bore da Cymru), although this delightful church with its feet in the river is very much English and has been a place of worship for a thousand years. Time and again the atmosphere draws me back. Once, having returned several days later after a visit with my mother, I found her limoge enamel brooch in the grass among the gravestones where she had dropped it. What luck. But my mother thinks I am a witch.

A peewit project is being carried out locally with three or four farms experimenting with spring sowing so that the corn is not too long and wet to fatally soak the chicks.

MELVERLEY
St. Peters Church
SJ 332.165

76

© Maggie Humphry

A stunning building but I don't know why the stocks are upstairs. A bit of public humiliation might do good to those with antisocial behaviour.

"Bring back the stocks"?

| 78 | **MUCH WENLOCK**
 the Guildhall
 SO 624.999 |

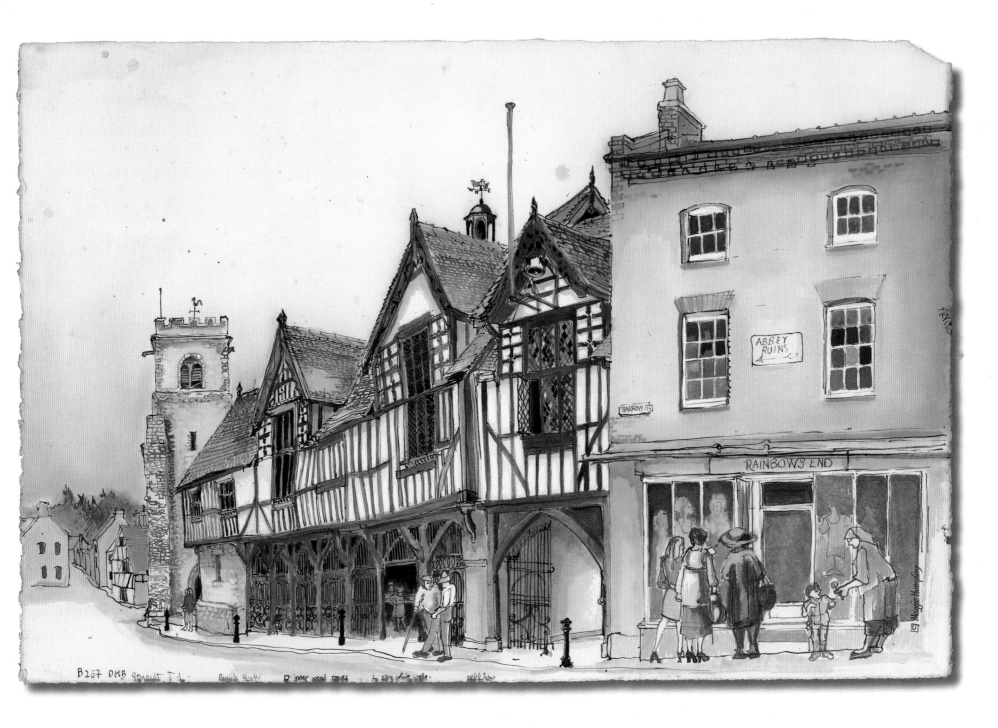

ABBEY RUINS

BARROW ST

RAINBOWS END

B267 DMB Renault T.1.   Pamela Hunter   R inner wood rowes   L sky white walls   brickwork

Agile dormice thrive in the woods of Wenlock Edge. On the lower slopes orchids and wild flowers grow in abundance on the limestone. Periodically the Shropshire Wildlife Trust harvests the seeds of Marked Ash meadows rich in flora to sow on less fruitful land to be converted to hay fields.

80	MUCH WENLOCK
	houses
	SO 620.997

My old yearning to live on a farm long gone, I now feast my eyes and capture the traditional buildings soon to be converted. What of the swallows, owls, and secret creatures? Countless dark recesses smelling of hay and animals soon to be lost. A moving figure in the gloom attracts the ever hungry sheep.

Giant puff balls grow in fairy rings waiting to be plucked from the turf and fried for tea — yum, yum.

82	**MUCKLEY CROSS** Barns SO 646.960

Maggie Humphry 2008

Locomotives and artefacts of the steam era are being skillfully restored by the dedicated men who work here. Engines, carriages, carts, barrows and lamps are being returned to their former glory. The rollingstock steam in and out so infrequently that the lizards live undisturbed in the ballast between the sleepers.

84	**OSWESTRY**
	the Cambrian Railway Museum
	SJ 294.298

Britain has 80% of the veteran trees of Europe, espcially in Shropshire. The Yew at Preen is reputed to be 1,547 years old and the oldest tree in Europe.

From prechristian times the English archers made their long bows from yew and practised their skill in the church yards. You can see the grooves on many of our churches where they sharpened their arrow heads.

| 86 | **PREEN** Manor House SO 542.982 |

Maggie Humphry

457 AD - YEW oldest in Europe

A special place on a sandstone outcrop. I should like to be buried here but the grave digger says the sandstone makes for a hard job up on that ridge.

Above me the nesting rooks scrapping, flapping and shouting in the spring made for a really noisy drawing. They use a grave like a water trough, drinking and splashing and arguing in raucous voices. What would Min Benbow think if she could hear all the commotion 6 feet above her head?

But twilight brings the rustling of the shy ones who creep about under the moon.

The church walls are made of tufa (a kind of limestone). You can still see it being formed in the Severn Valley Country Park at Alveley

88	**QUATFORD** the Church of ST. Mary Magdalene SO 738.908

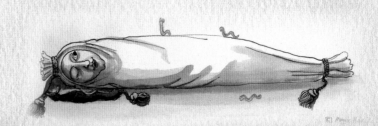

Shortly before moving to Shropshire I chanced upon this scene. White marguerites tumbled down the slope and yellow hammers flitted about the hedge. "This is the county for me" I thought. Later I turned my drawing into a 'Samuel Palmer' for a theme exhibition.

Formed by the cascading of shore line waves this solid little hill of Kenley grit had been settled long before the birth of Christianity. If you sat on the timber framed bellcote you could look down on the river Severn as it meanders across the flood plain of Leech Meadow where dozens of Canada geese often graze with the sheep.

SAMUEL PALMER

| 90 | **SHEINTON**
the church of St. Peter and St. Paul
SJ 611. 039 |

Maggie Humphry

St. James has long stood in one of the untouched villages which lie like sleepy pearls along the string of Corfdale. Some of their churches are 1,300 years old. Churchyards with their long grass, brambles and wildflowers are wonderful havens for wild life. I don't like manicured graveyards.

When I see the grass is long I know that I shall hear a thrush sing, as there will be plenty of snails, which are one of the thrush's favourite foods. The broken shells can be seen where the thrush taps them on a chosen stone. I never, ever use slug pellets as the thrush too will eat the poison of the dying snail.

| 92 | **SHIPTON**
Church of St. James
SO 562 . 918 |

Their usual island washed aside by one of the terrible floods, whose treacherous dark waters have so often flowed into cellars, vaults and buildings of lower Shrewsbury, the swans of English Bridge have moved upstream to nest.

Sitting by a Welsh river (the Clwyd) one hot summers day, a kingfisher flashed past with a fish in its mouth. Knowing it was feeding chicks it took me three days to find its nest in the bank. Climbing into the river at twilight I shone a torch into the tunnel to see the chicks lined up. After being fed at the front they move to the back of the queue. I spent an indulgent summer kingfisher watching

HURRY UP
IM STARVING

94 **SHREWSBURY**
the English Bridge
SJ 496 . 123

© Maggie Humphry

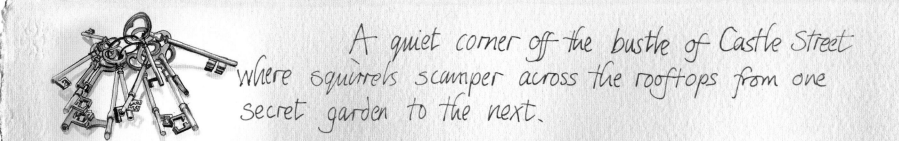

A quiet corner off the bustle of Castle Street where squirrels scamper across the rooftops from one secret garden to the next.

96	**SHREWSBURY** The Gatehouse SJ 494.127

12.15   10.45-1.30   1610   spourds on gutter   David Jenkins. Backs on River   Maggie Humphry

The first building in Shropshire into which I went. Nonsmoking but the beer must be good as the smokers go outside for a puff before returning to their pints. I once borrowed a long ladder from the obliging landlord (who had fishes printed all over his trousers). The ducking customers jovially passed it through the low ceilinged bar.

I HAVE SPAT IN THIS BEER

98	**SHREWSBURY** Three Fishes pub
	SJ 493 . 125

Those who know Telford well can show you the gems of medieval architecture hiding in the old villages of which the new town is made. Built in 1653, Stirchley Hall is one such historic building. The old cart has found a resting place, adding character and bringing to mind 'Cider with Rosie' in the hay meadows before trundling home to fill the barns. Hay still grows in the fields here, where grass snakes continue to hunt the frogs.

100	STIRCHLEY HALL
	SJ 698.067

There is a magic in the wooded hills which flows and fills the valley, hinting at different times. So old. So old. The walls once echoing with tales and laughter and much good sweet wine filling the cups. Flanked by a sea of yellow rape and rippling corn this great stone ship comes sailing down. Brambles and wild oats are pushed aside like ocean waves.

102	**STOKESAY** Castle
	SO 436.816

Brimming with animals and children. I cannot imagine a more idyllic setting for childhood. The orchards hang with apples, the Rayburn is full of pies and the wren nests under the eves.

THE SMITHIES

104 | Round Hill Farm

©Maggie Humphry

sheep chickens & children everywhere

Whilst designing the gardens in nearby Weston Park, Capability Brown built this dovecot which stands solidly in a farmyard near Tong. You can see it with ease from the M54 if you're travelling south by coach, but not by car.

106	**TONG** Vauxhall Farm SJ 783.076

Maggie Humphry

Waves of roof tiles flow over the eyebrow windows which peer out at the winter world. The skeletal holly has seen many a good Christmas.

Peacefully fishing in nearby pools the great crested grebe bobs up long distances from where it dived, whilst in summer reed buntings call incessantly from the damp undergrowth.

| 108 | **TONG**
Shoemakers' Cottage
SJ 796.075 |

BIRCH

holly tree seen many xmas..   alsatian with back legs down - flies throwing   Shoe maker   Chilton - old long house

© Maggie Humphry

Bathed in brilliant sunshine, the whole world seemed to open up with the promise of a new summer just around the corner, and I heard the evocative call of the first cuckoo of spring. For 59 years this garden brought a magnitude of joys to the same tending hand.

110	**WESTBURY** A Cottage SJ 353.096

I heard the 1ST cuckoo   Kensington Rd.   © Maggie Humphry

Having just been restored, this mechanism from Newton church in South Wales ticks methodically over the test pit of Joyce's clock works.

Famous for clocks and the nursery rhymes of Randolph Caldecott what else does one think of but Hickory Dickory Dock? But it should be the water vole running up the clock as they flourish here. Although they have declined nationally because of mink. The best place to see them is in Stags Brook at the back of the supermarket car park.

WHAT TIME DO YOU CALL THIS?

112	**WHITCHURCH** Workshop of J.B. Joyce and co. SJ 547.415

©Maggie Humphry

Last dance for the garden frogs - by Marilyn Gunn

Fat ballerinas
winter trapped you
under its crystal lid.

No pirouettes then
just one last dance
slowed to a few cold turns
folding you down and in
like dying swans.

You won't be princes now
whoever comes warm-hearted
with a kiss.

Just skin and bloat
still softly buoyed and floating
with your phied knees
your trailing graceless feet.

| 114 | **WHITTINGTON**
Castle
SJ 325.311 |

A flat, flat land of horizontal ribbons tied each end of the landscape, cupped over by an enormous sky.

For 40 winters Abbie has bent his back to cut the dark peat. In former times over 50 voices chatted and sang across the bog, and the loaded train steamed away with its brown harvest. Now, with his son, he is the last of the peat cutters.

Two solitary figures working in unison down the lines. Their wide pattens paddling like ducks feet on the wet peat. In many years, when they are under turf, the mosses, now a nature reserve, will revert to the raised bog that began to form 10,000 years ago.

Kestrels hover (how he rung upon the rein of a wimpling wing in his ecstacy!) and the sigh of the wind in the cotton grass.

(Actually, looking at the map I think Fenn's Moss, where I drew this, is just a few yards inside Wales — but don't tell anyone!)

| 116 | **WHIXALL** Fenns Moss SJ 491.357 |

© Maggie Humphry

This magnificent hall nestles in the valley with picturesque cottages and a stately sandstone church whose spire reaches up to the woods behind. A taste of eternal summer when lilies and roses fill the air with lingering scent. In lush water gardens behind, the stream trickles endlessly, dragonflies dart among the lilies whilst crayfish creep in the mud. Well loved gardens delicately tended.

118	WORFIELD Lower Hall. SO 757.958

Maggie Humphry

Under the watchful eye of the Wrekin grapes have been harvested from these in vineyards since Roman times.

Angry with the residents, a giant was intending to block the river and flood the people of Shrewsbury. The shoemender from Wellington, when asked the way by the giant, said "I have worn out all these shoes out returning from Shrewsbury". So thinking he had far, far too many miles to walk the tricked giant jumped his load where he stood — and lo, behold the Wrekin.

© Maggie Humphry

Silver moon bathing barns in silver light and silver owls hunt silently.

	WYKE
122	Wyke farm
	SJ 648.020

Maggie Humphry

Shropshire Wildlife Trust

We all love our county, and Maggie's book will help people to love and appreciate it even more. Although most of her main pictures are of buildings, she's keenly aware of the importance that nature has as a source of pleasure, and as a provider of the essential balance between ourselves and our environment. Wildlife is one of her great passions.

A major rôle of the Shropshire Wildlife Trust is help people discover and enjoy the wonderful range of opportunities that nature provides in the county. It's the only charity dedicated to conserving species and habitats, and it needs members, volunteers, and even money to achieve its aims - hence our pleasure at being associated with this fund raising book.

Maggie's book and our activities

Three times a year the Trust's members receive our own attractive magazine, "Shropshire Wildlife". Along with informative and enjoyable reviews, pictures, and project updates, there's a regular diary section. Dozens of walks, special projects and other events are listed - and many of them involve the things that Maggie's mentioned or drawn.

There are opportunities to see bats, bees, wasps and butterflies. We have special places where you can come to observe frogs and toads and newts. You can visit fens and bogs, help us with our work on high hills, and come to places where coppicing still goes on. For those who are interested in nature-past we have geology trips, looking at old land formations and the relics of plants and animals long gone, revealed by fossils.

Our activities and your future

Children and young people are a particular focus for the Trust's activities. Their health, well-being and quality of life will improve through contact with wildlife. All children are fascinated by nature, given the chance. The Trust is concerned to provide that chance, and to interest and attract children to wildlife pursuits, and to educate them in the need to retain biodiversity, for everybody's sake.

Thousands came on trips to our nature reserves during the last year. We've established Wildlife Watch Groups across the county. Scores of parents and their children have been involved in our projects, like planting thousands of heathers on the Stiperstones as part of our "Back to Purple" scheme, and tiny tots taking part in a "Forest School" pilot scheme, including tree climbing and making dens.

Whetted your appetite? Want to know more? Want to join?

Come to our delightful shop and visitor centre in Abbey Foregate in Shrewsbury.

Ring us on 01743-284280

Visit our website at www.shropshirewildlifetrust.org.uk

THE wildlife TRUSTS

Maggie's other work

This book gives you a really good taste of Maggie's drawing and watercolouring skill, but she also works enthusiastically in oil. Her style in that medium is quite different, but her thoroughness is consistent. The landscape is of Burgui in Northern Spain, and the portrait is "Music Maker".

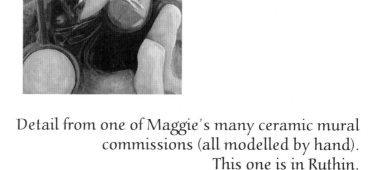

Maggie learned her basic etching skills with John Brunsdon at St. Albans. Since moving away from her ceramics work, she's spent a lot of time redeveloping and extending her skills in authographic printing. "Wrekin Fan" is a collagraph whose plate was made up from leaves collected from around Shropshire's most well known hill. "Moonflock" is an etching.

Detail from one of Maggie's many ceramic mural commissions (all modelled by hand). This one is in Ruthin.

This acylic with gold leaf icon is called "1403". It was one of the two pieces accepted for the Sotheby's 2003 Open in Shrewsbury, the theme for which was the Battle of Shrewsbury, and Conflict. A totally different medium, but a wholly predictable dedication to form, content, and style.

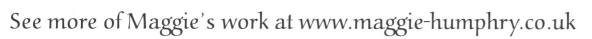

See more of Maggie's work at www.maggie-humphry.co.uk

Making more of Maggie's Shropshire scenes

Not only can you make this delightful book even more "your own" by adding your own comments, observations, and sketches, but each of the sixty main images can be bought as prints.

All but the three shown here are available on A4 paper, with a cream coloured mount. Each mount is signed by Maggie. The overall size is 40.5 by 30.5 cm. These prints are £14.95 each.

The three on the right are available as high quality reproduction prints in editions of 250, price £25 each : Muckley Cross (82), Stokesay (102), and Worfield (118). They are unmounted, numbered & signed, and printed with lightfast inks on heavyweight acid-free watercolour-equivalent paper (45 by 32 cm). The approximate sizes of the images are : Muckley and Stokesay, 32 by 23 cm : Worfield 41 by 26 cm.

To order

By post ... copy the order form below, and send it with payment to
GET Services, The Old Fire Engine Station, High Street, Bridgnorth. WV16 4DB

Telephone : 01746-766477   Fax : 01746
E-mail : shropshire@getservices   online at www.getservices.org.uk/shropshire

Please order all items on this page from ...
• www.look-at-book.com
• or Maggie at The Pink House, 23 King Street, Broseley. ☎ 01952-881037
TF12 5NA

Picture title & number		each	Total price
			£
		£	£
		£	£
		£	£
	P & P	£1.95	£

Signature _____

I enclose cheque/postal order payable to GET Services Ltd for £
OR
Please debit my Mastercard / Visa / Switch / Amex

Card number _ _ _ _ _ _ _ _ _ _ _ _ _ _ _ _

Expiry date _ _ _ _   Issue number (switch only) _ _

Card verification number _ _ _   (last three digits on signature strip)

Name _____

Address _____

_____

Postcode _____   Telephone _____